For Maria, Ian and Rachel Kirkbride
W.M.

For Maggie
B.F.

First published 1987 by
Walker Books Ltd
184-192 Drummond Street
London NW1 3HP

Text © 1987 William Mayne
Illustrations © 1987 Barbara Firth

First printed 1987
Printed and bound by
L.E.G.O., Vicenza, Italy

British Library Cataloguing in Publication Data
Mayne, William
Leapfrog.—(Animal library)
1. Readers—1950-
1. Title   II. Firth, Barbara   III. Series
428.6   PE1119

ISBN 0-7445-0726-X

Leapfrog

Written by
William Mayne

Illustrated by
Barbara Firth

WALKER BOOKS
LONDON

In Tadpole Town the water is warm.
Rowley stretches himself one day in his jelly
egg and splits the side.

"Out we go," he says, and wriggles free.
He thinks he is alone in the water.

"I'm glad you're here," says a little voice.
"I thought I was the only one."

There is a girl tadpole, Sally. Rowley
thinks she is the most beautiful tadpole he has
ever seen, and of course she is. She has
eyelashes.

"You are so handsome," she says to him.
"What a fine tail."

"Do you think so?" he says, so pleased.

The spawn begins to shake. It is only jelly.
Out come boys and girls, running up and
down the streets of Tadpole Town.
Other people living there are upset.

Old Beetle is bowled over.
Spiders grumble in their silver bubbles.
Mosquito babies swim for their lives.
Even the mud is grumpy.

The sunshine keeps all the tadpoles warm.

Boy tadpoles come to look at Sally. She is special. But she only cares for Rowley. They stay together by their careful friend, wise old Mussel in his shell.

"How good to be tadpoles," says Rowley. "I'm glad I'm not a boatman with skating legs."

At the top of the water boatmen skim about.

"Legs are disgusting," says Sally. "Head and tail are all we need."

"Hurrah for heads and tails," say all the tadpoles.

One day the sun does not shine.
The top of the water is not smooth
any more, but wrinkly. Boatmen
sink. Rowley wriggles up
to see what blinds the sky.

Drops of cold water are falling from a
cloud. Rowley puts his nose out and it's
funny stuff up there, so thin and
dry it makes him sneeze.

He wriggles down again to tell Sally.
It is a long way to the bottom. The
water in Tadpole Town is cold.
Sally is not there.
"Sally," he calls.

Wise old Mussel opens his shell and looks out. "Too much noise," he says. "You'll bring Fish."
"Where is Sally?" asks Rowley.
"Gone," says Mussel. "We're having Flood. All this cold water is Flood, and it's washed her away. She's gone."

"Let's go and get her," says Rowley.

"Your average mussel is not a travelling man," says Mussel. "You'll have to go alone, up to overflow and out. But quick; Flood is nearly over, and if Snake hasn't got her then Heron has, or Eel, or worst of all, Boy."

Rowley wriggles up. It is a long way across to overflow. Tadpole Town is in a bigger pond now.

Rowley begins to swim properly. It is the fastest way to go.

It is not fast enough. By the time he gets to overflow Flood has finished and the drain is dry.

While he looks the sun comes out again.

There is a sharp shadow. The sharp shadow comes towards him.

It is Heron's shadow, wanting him for food. He swims right out of the water into the dry drain and escapes.

He is out of the water and cannot
swim. He wriggles in the air and flips from
side to side.

A long thing follows him down the drain
and opens its mouth. There are two pointed
teeth with poison. It is Snake. Snake likes
Tadpole when Snake is hungry.

Rowley somersaults. There is
no water to breathe, so he drinks
some air. He runs away.
"I cannot do that," he thinks. "I have no legs."
Snake hisses and goes away. Snake does not
approve of legs either.

Beyond the dry drain lies the brook.

Rowley tumbles in and to the bottom. He finds a comfortable place to rest. Something comes out of the comfortable place, waves many legs, bites his tail and shouts at him to go away. It is Caddis.

"I'm sorry," says Rowley. "Have you seen Sally anywhere?"

Caddis goes into his burrow and crawls away with it, saying not a word.

Rowley finds another place,
but this time prickly Fish bites his tail. Rowley
kicks and kicks to get away from his bad
temper. He has truly grown legs now.
 Crayfish puts out a grabbing claw but does
not get him. Rowley thinks he could have
eaten Sally, but it is no good asking
Crayfish anything at all.

Rowley hopes he has not grown
legs like that. "Head and tail are best,"
he remembers. "I hope Sally does not mind
that I'm so ugly now, if I ever find her."

He asks gentle Fish, all sleepy in
the stream, "Have you seen Sally?"
  "Come closer," says gentle, lazy Fish.
"I'm a little deaf. Come closer still and
closer. Pop your head inside my mouth.
Now come right in. Aah."
  When Fish says "Aah"
Rowley leaps backwards,
out of the water,
into the air.

"How fine and fresh," he thinks. "I'll fly. And
what great back legs I have." He plops down
into the water and sits there with his nose out.

"Breathing air," he says. "I've gone off water."
He sits and waits, a long way now
from Tadpole Town.

A voice speaks to him.
"Can it be Rowley?" it asks.

He looks round. No one is there but a sort
of Lizard, and some Snails, but Snails can't talk.

"Good afternoon," says Rowley, very polite,
because it is a pretty and a golden Lizard. But
he finds his voice is very croaky.

"Oh," says the Lizard, "have you forgotten me? I'm Sally. But I don't expect you want to speak to me now."

"How you've changed," says Rowley. "But I don't mind, because you are even more beautiful, so gold, so smooth, so smart, and I can almost see through you."

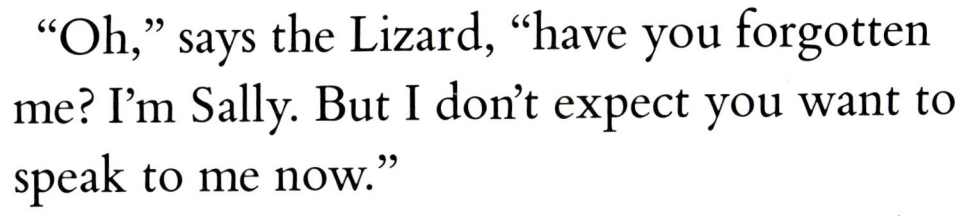

He thinks how ugly his legs are now, and that he has no tail at all. Something in his throat makes his voice dark, and there is no wriggle left in him.

He begins to swim away, a tear in his eye, sure she will hate him.

Two things happen. Huge hungry Eel
comes up the brook and sets his eyes on Sally,
straightens his fins, opens his mouth of sixty
teeth in a smile. It is not admiration but greed.

And sharp shadow falls again on Rowley.
"Sally for Eel, Rowley for Heron," he thinks.
Sally does not see Eel because she is looking
at Rowley.

Rowley turns about, throws away his tears,
and pushes Sally under a safe stone.

Heron stabs down, misses him,
catches Eel and flies off with that.
  "Rowley, so brave, so handsome,
with fine arms and legs so green," says Sally.
  "Oh, Sally," says Rowley, and sees that she
has golden legs too.
    Together at last, keeping a look-out for
Boy, they sit on a lily leaf side by side,
green Frog and golden Newt.